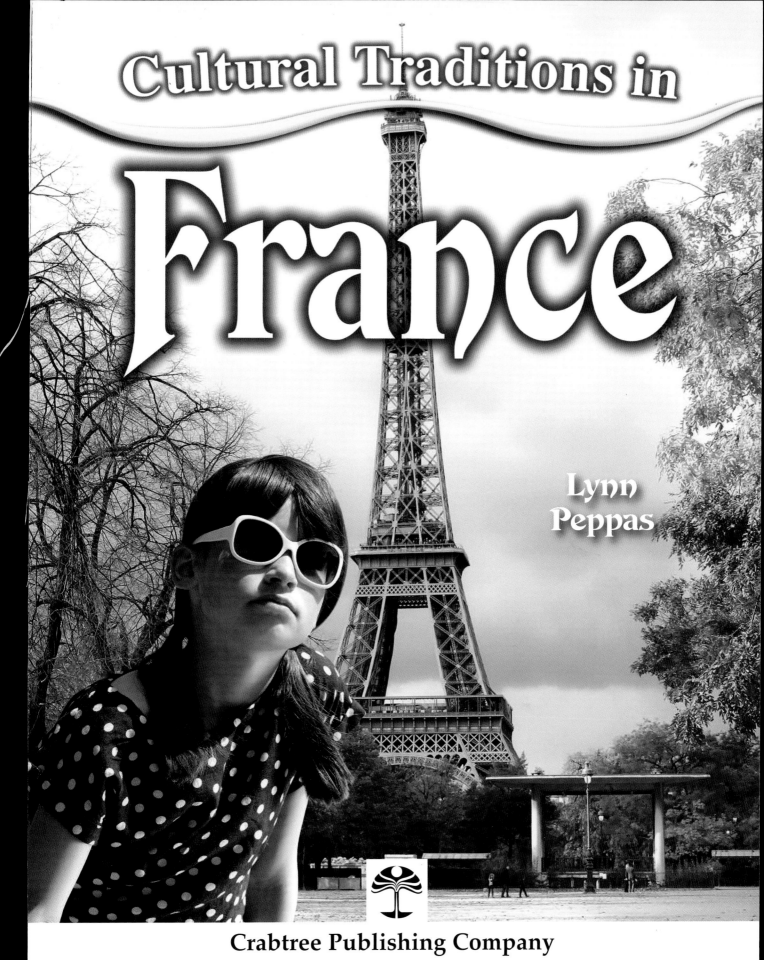

Cultural Traditions in France

Lynn Peppas

Crabtree Publishing Company

www.crabtreebooks.com

Crabtree Publishing Company

www.crabtreebooks.com

Author: Lynn Peppas
Publishing plan research and development:
   Reagan Miller
Editor: Crystal Sikkens
Proofreaders: Janice Dyer, Wendy Scavuzzo
Indexer: Wendy Scavuzzo
Design: Tibor Choleva
Photo research: Melissa McClellan
Production coordinator and prepress technician:
   Tammy McGarr
Print coordinator: Margaret Amy Salter

Produced and Designed by BlueAppleWorks Inc.

Cover: bourguignonne snail au gratin (bottom center);
Paris woman eating macaroon (center); Notre dame de
Paris - France (background); French Baguette (bottom
left); Blue Colored Iris Flowers (left middle, right top,
and bottom); The Thinker by Auguste Rodin (right
center); Brie (bottom)

Title page: Eiffel Tower Paris

Illustrations:
Barbara Bedell: page 29

Photographs:
Dreamstime: © Outline205: page 1; © Richard Griffin:
   page 15 (bottom)
Keystone Press: ZUMAPRESS page 7; Audureau Aurelie/
   KPA-ZUMA © 2006 by Maxppp: page 11 (bottom)
Shutterstock: Cover (all): © marco mayer (bottom center);
   © Ariwasabi (center); © Perig (background); © Kittichai (bottom
   left); © Vilor (left middle, right top and bottom); © Toniflap (right
   center); © Khutornaia Svetlana (bottom); © 75tiks: page 1 (bottom);
   © pavalena: page 4 (left); © William Perugini: page 4 (right); ©
   K.N.V.: pages 6–7 (top); © bonchan: page 6 (middle);
   © Patrick Wang: page 6 (bottom); © Anna Breitenberger: pages 8-9
   (background); © Nathalie Speliers Ufermann: page 9 (left); © Ufuk
   ZIVANA page 10 (top); © Oliver Hoffmann: page 11 (inset);
   © Tupungato: page 12; © oksmit: page 12 (middle); © Syda
   Productions: page 12 (bottom); © DBtale: page 13 (bottom); ©
   Brian S: page 14; © bikeriderlondon: page 15 (top); © Aaron
   Amat: page 16 (inset); © lotsostock: page 16; © Evgeny Prokofyev:
   page 17; © Monkey Business Images: pages 18, 19 (inset); ©
   oliveromg: page 19; © Natalia Barsukova: page 20 (background); ©
   Migel: page 21; © Doin Oakenhelm: page 22; © sigurcamp: page 23;
   © Pecold: page 24; © Nick_Nick: page 26; © Felix-Andrei
   Constantinescu: page 28; © sansa55: page 30
SuperStock: Photononstop: pages 10 (bottom), 25; age fotostock:
   page 29 (bottom)
Wikimedia Commons: Creative Commons: page 18 (inset);
   Thesupermat: page 27; Jebulon: page 28 (inset); Public Domain:
   pages 5, 13 (top), 26, 31 (top, inset, bottom), 20

Library and Archives Canada Cataloguing in Publication

Peppas, Lynn, author
   Cultural traditions in France / Lynn Peppas.

(Cultural traditions in my world)
Includes index.
Issued in print and electronic formats.
ISBN 978-0-7787-0302-0 (bound).--ISBN 978-0-7787-0314-3 (pbk.).--
ISBN 978-1-4271-7486-4 (html).--ISBN 978-1-4271-7492-5 (pdf)

   1. Holidays--France--Juvenile literature. 2. France--Social life
and customs--Juvenile literature. I. Title. II. Series: Cultural
traditions in my world

GT4849.A2P46 2014   j394.26944   C2014-900907-0
                                       C2014-900908-9

Library of Congress Cataloging-in-Publication Data

Peppas, Lynn.
   Cultural traditions in France / Lynn Peppas.
      pages cm. -- (Cultural traditions in my world)
   Includes index.
   ISBN 978-0-7787-0302-0 (reinforced library binding : alk. paper) -- ISBN 978-0-
7787-0314-3 (pbk. : alk. paper) -- ISBN 978-1-4271-7492-5 (electronic pdf : alk.
paper) -- ISBN 978-1-4271-7486-4 (electronic html : alk. paper)
   1. Holidays--France--Juvenile literature. 2. Festivals--France--Juvenile
literature. 3. France--Social life and customs--Juvenile literature. I. Title.

GT4849.A2P47 2014
394.26944--dc23
                              2014005115

Crabtree Publishing Company

www.crabtreebooks.com   1-800-387-7650

Printed in the USA/052014/SN20140313

Published in Canada
Crabtree Publishing
616 Welland Ave.
St. Catharines, ON
L2M 5V6

Published in the United States
Crabtree Publishing
PMB 59051
350 Fifth Avenue, 59th Floor
New York, New York 10118

Published in the United Kingdom
Crabtree Publishing
Maritime House
Basin Road North, Hove
BN41 1WR

Published in Australia
Crabtree Publishing
3 Charles Street
Coburg North
VIC 3058

Contents

Welcome to France!

France is a country in Europe. It has a rich culture of **traditions** and celebrations that have been followed for many years. The west coast of France is beside the Atlantic Ocean. The eastern border of France is beside the European countries of Germany, Switzerland, and Italy. Belgium and the English Channel are north of France. Spain and the Mediterranean Sea lie to the south. Over 65 million people live in France.

The capital of France is Paris. Many believe that Paris is the most romantic city in the world!

France is a **multicultural** nation where many different cultures and religions are practiced. The majority of religious people practice **Christianity**, however, religions such as **Judaism** and **Islam** are also practiced. The country's official language is French. Millions of people travel to France for its delicious food and exciting festivals. Many of the country's celebrations are based on the Christian religion.

Did You Know?
France's beautiful landscapes have inspired famous artists. Vincent van Gogh's painting, *The Starry Night*, is based on the French region Saint-Rémy-de-Provence.

New Year's

New Year's Day (Jour de l'an) is celebrated on the first day of the New Year, January 1. In France it is a public holiday. A public holiday is a day when most people get the day off work or school. People get together with friends or family members and watch fireworks displays at midnight on New Year's Eve, the night before New Year's Day. The French sing famous New Year's songs, such as "Auld Lang Syne" ("Choral des Adieux"), but with French words.

One traditional New Year's Day food is the King Cake. A coin or bean is often baked inside and the person who finds it is crowned King for the day.

Both children and adults take part in picking grapes at midnight in Viella.

In some areas of France, people take part in different traditions. In a small town in southern France called Viella, people go to church on New Year's Eve. After church they walk to the nearby **vineyards**. Torchlights are lit and people pick the grapes at midnight. From these grapes they make a special New Year's wine. People have been enjoying this tradition since the 1990s.

Mardi Gras

Mardi Gras is a Christian holiday that means Fat Tuesday in English. This celebration falls on a Tuesday between February 3 and March 9. It is always 47 days before Easter. Mardi Gras is traditionally a day of feasting before the period of **fasting** begins that leads up to Easter.

Did You Know?
The period of fasting leading up to Easter is known as **Lent**. Lent begins on **Ash Wednesday**, the day after Mardi Gras.

In France, Mardi Gras is celebrated by eating rich foods such as pancakes, waffles, or crépes.

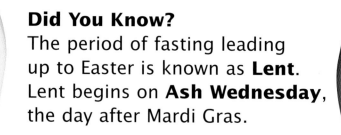

Mardi Gras is not only celebrated with food, but also entertainment. The famous festival known as Carnival began in Nice 800 years ago. This festival includes colorful parades with large floats, musicians, and dancers in colorful costumes. One popular parade during Nice's Carnival is the Flower Parade. The floats and costumes are decorated with real flowers. Flowers are thrown into the crowd of **spectators**.

The three-week long Nice Carnival ends on Mardi Gras.

Easter in France

Easter is a Christian holiday that falls on a different date every year. It is celebrated on a Sunday between March 22 and April 25. Christians celebrate Easter Sunday as the day that Jesus Christ returned to life after his death. They believe Jesus died on Good Friday, the Friday before Easter. Church bells do not ring on Good Friday. On Easter Sunday, the bells, known as Easter Bells, ring loudly to celebrate Jesus' life after death.

Special church services are held on Easter Sunday and the week leading up to Easter known as Holy Week.

Many families in France share a big Easter dinner with friends and family. Lamb is the traditional meat served. In the Alsace region of France, special cookies called *Osterlammele* are eaten to celebrate Easter. They are shaped like lambs. These cookies were first introduced to the area by the Germans over 100 years ago.

Osterlammele

Did You Know?
Many children believe that the Easter Bells leave the churches on Good Friday. They return on Easter Sunday and drop gifts such as chocolate bells, bunnies, and eggs for children to find.

April Fish!

In France, April Fish (Poisson d'Avril) falls on the first day of April. It is very much like the North American celebration called April Fool's Day. In France, people try to attach a paper fish onto another person's back without it being noticed. The person wearing the fish on their back gives chocolate-candy fish to the person who pulled the prank on them.

When the fish is finally noticed, people call out "Poisson d'Avril" (April Fish)!

The April Fish celebration began over 400 years ago. Some people believe that the French used to celebrate New Year's Day on April 1 until France's King Charles IX changed it to January 1. People who did not like this change and who continued to celebrate on April 1 had jokes played on them. But the truth is that no one really knows why the celebration started.

King Charles IX became the King of France when he was only ten years old.

Did You Know? Sometimes the **media** make up false news stories on April Fish that they share with readers and viewers. The next day they reveal the truth. It is all a part of the trick-playing on April Fish!

French chocolate-candy fish is a great-tasting treat.

Labor Day

In France, Labor Day (Fête du Travail) or May Day (La Fête du Muguet) is a public holiday that is celebrated on the first day of May. Government offices, businesses, banks, and most stores are closed for the holiday. Labor Day celebrates workers and workers' rights. People take part in parades and marches on this day.

Drummers and other musicians often take part in Labor Day parades in France. Over 80 other countries in the world celebrate Labor Day on May 1. The day is also known as **International** Workers' Day.

Long ago, Labor Day and May Day were separate holidays. May Day celebrated the coming of spring. At that time, the king of France was given Lily-of-the-Valley flowers on the first day of May. He liked it so much that he started the tradition by giving others Lily-of-the-Valley flowers on May 1, too. When other countries started celebrating Labor Day at the beginning of May, France decided to combine the two holidays and celebrate both on the same day.

Did You Know?
Many French people pin a Dog Rose flower to their clothing for good luck on May Day.

Victory in Europe Day

Victory in Europe Day (Fête de la Victoire) is a national holiday when the French celebrate the end of World War II. A national holiday is a day when people of one country celebrate their nation's history. Victory in Europe Day is held on May 8 because it was on this date that the end of World War II was declared in France. Most people get the day off work or school.

The French show their patriotism, or love for their country, by flying France's flag.

World War II was fought between two groups: the Allies and the Axis powers. France joined with the Allied countries but had to surrender to the Axis countries, including Germany, on June 25, 1940. German forces **occupied** France for four years until the Axis powers were defeated at the end of the war. On Victory in Europe Day, the French honor those who bravely fought for their freedom.

Did You Know?
Victory in Europe Day did not become an official public holiday until 1981—over 35 years after the war ended!

Many people gather to watch military parades that take place in cities throughout France on Victory in Europe Day.

Mother's Day and Father's Day

The last Sunday in May is a special day that children honor their mothers for all the things they do. Families gather for a special dinner and often moms are given gifts on Mother's Day. For some moms, it is a day to relax and not do any work.

Did You Know?
On Mother's Day, many mother's in France also receive a special cake that looks like a bouquet of flowers.

Fathers also get a special day in France. Starting in 1952, the third Sunday in June was declared Father's Day. As with mothers, fathers are often presented with gifts and a special dinner is prepared in their honor. Homemade crafts, cards, or chocolates are common gifts for dads.

Father's Day falls at the beginning of summer. Some families plan outdoor activities with their dads, such as picnics or barbecues.

French National Day

French National Day (La Fête Nationale) is often called Bastille Day by English-speaking people. It celebrates the anniversary of the beginning of the French Revolution. A revolution happens when citizens of a country come together to throw out their government by using violence. The French Revolution started because the citizens disagreed with how the king was governing France. On July 14, 1789, they attacked the Bastille, which is a fort and prison in Paris.

French artist, Jean-Pierre Houël, witnessed the attack on the Bastille in 1789. He painted this picture the same year.

Members of the French air force fly aircraft above the military parade in Paris.

Today, the French watch military parades on Bastille Day. The most famous military parade takes place in Paris along a street called the Champs-Élysées. The day ends with fireworks in many cities in France. People often take part in public dances on this day.

Did You Know?
The French Revolution changed France's government from a monarchy—where a king is the only ruler—to a republic—where elected officials govern.

Assumption of the Blessed Virgin Mary

On August 15, the French celebrate the Assumption of the Blessed Virgin Mary (l'Assomption de la Vierge Marie). This Christian holiday honors Mary, the mother of Jesus Christ. Christians celebrate the day that Mary rose to heaven and was joined again with her son Jesus.

Did You Know?
In 1858, Bernadette Soubirous from Lourdes, France, was visited by the Virgin Mary 18 times. Because of this, many churches and monuments in Lourdes were built in honor of the Virgin Mary.

Flowers are laid at the base of this monument of the Virgin Mary in Lourdes, France.

Christians carry a statue of the Virgin Mary through the streets of Marseille, France, on August 15.

People attend special church services on Assumption Day. Many towns and cities throughout France hold festivals to honor Mary. One tradition involves priests, nuns, and other Christians parading through the streets carrying a statue of the Virgin Mary. Some people carry the statue to a boat and ride down the Seine River.

All Saints' Day

All Saints' Day (La Toussaint) is a religious holiday that is celebrated by Christians throughout the world on November 1. A saint is a person who has lived a holy life in the eyes of the Christian officials. All Saints' Day—as the name suggests—honors the lives of all saints.

French Christians celebrate the lives of all the saints—the ones who are littleknown as well as those who are well-known!

Flowers are often left at gravesites on All Saints' Day.

On All Saints' Day, many Christians in France attend special church services. It is also a day when many families visit cemeteries to remember loved ones who are buried there.

Did You Know?
Over 500 years ago in France, the dead were remembered the day after All Saints' Day, on November 2. Today, since many have November 1 off work, people visit the gravesites of loved ones on All Saints' Day instead.

Armistice Day

Armistice Day (L'Armistice de la Première Guerre Mondiale) is a national holiday that is held in France on November 11. It is a day for people to show their respect and give thanks to the millions of men and women who fought in various wars on behalf of France.

Did You Know?
Other countries around the world honor this day, too. In Canada, the holiday is called Remembrance Day. In the United States, it is called Veterans Day.

In France, over one million soldiers gave their lives in World War I. World War I ended on November 11, 1918.

Similar to other countries, the French honor their soldiers in various ways. Flags are flown at half-mast, or partway down the flagpole, to show respect for the dead. After one-minute of silence, church bells are rung around the country. Red poppies are worn to show respect for the soldiers. Ceremonies are held at war memorials and battlefields. Wreaths or flowers are laid at these sites to honor those who have died.

An unidentified French soldier from World War I was buried beneath the Arc de Triomphe monument in Paris on November 11, 1920. This soldier is a symbol of all the soldiers who died during the war. A flame lit in 1923 still burns on the tomb today.

Christmas in France

Most places in France celebrate Christmas on December 25. For many, the holiday includes family reunions, midnight mass, a big Christmas dinner, and a visit from Père Noël. Midnight mass is a church service held at 12 a.m. on December 24. Christians celebrate the birth of Jesus Christ at the start of His birthday on December 25. A traditional Christmas feast often takes place after the service.

Did You Know?
A popular Christmas decoration in France is the **nativity scene** of Jesus' birth.

La bûche de Noël, or a Yule log cake, is a traditional French Christmas dessert.

French children await the arrival of Père Noël on Christmas morning. Père Noël is similar to Santa Claus in North America. Children leave their shoes by the fireplace before bed on December 24 in hopes that Père Noël will fill them with small gifts and candies that night.

Père Noël might also hang small toys, fruit, or nuts on the Christmas tree for children Christmas morning.

Did You Know?
During the Christmas season, people can be heard greeting each other "Joyeux Noël," which means "Merry Christmas" in French.

Annual Festivals

France's popular festivals throughout the year add to its unique culture. The famous Cannes Film Festival (Festival de Cannes) brings people from all over the world to Cannes, France, every September. Famous celebrities, movie reviewers, and movie fans attend this festival to see films and documentaries before they are released in movie theaters. The first festival took place in 1946.

The Avignon Festival has taken place in Provence, France, since 1947. This festival celebrates live plays and theater.

The Festival of Music (Féte de la Musique) is held every year on World Music Day on June 21. Maurice Fleuret started the festival in Paris as a way to celebrate music in France's culture.

The Medieval Festival of Sedan celebrates France's history on a weekend in May. People wear medieval costumes and enjoy medieval music, food, and games. Sedan is also home to a medieval castle that was built in 1424.

Knights on horses take part in competitions called tournaments during the Medieval Festival of Sedan.

Glossary

Ash Wednesday The first day of Lent

Christianity A religion practiced by Christians that follows the teachings of Jesus Christ

customary A usual practice

fasting To not eat food; often for religious reasons

international Global or worldwide

Islam A religion practiced by Muslims that follows one God through the teachings of the prophet, Muhammad

Judaism A religion practiced by Jews that follows one God through the teachings of the Old Testament bible

Lent A religious practice when Christians give up certain foods for a period of 40 days to remember how Jesus suffered for them

media Sources of news and information given to the public through television, newspapers, internet, and radio

multicultural Made up of several cultural or ethnic groups

nativity scene A display of the manger in which Jesus was born

occupied Moved in and took over an area

patriotism Love of country

spectators People who watch a performance, or event

traditions Customs or beliefs that are passed down from generation to generation

vineyard A field where grapevines or crops are planted

Index